Leaf's Skin

seasoned poems

Leaf's Skin

seasoned poems

KUMAR ABHISHEK

illustrated by Sharon Lim Sautarel

First published in India in 2025 by Kumar Abhishek

ISBN 978-93-34151-95-4

BISAC: POE000000/POETRY/General

Cover artwork and illustrations by Sharon Lim Sautarel

Typesetting: CinnamonTeal Design and Publishing

Dedication

dedicated to my father,
to my family and readers,
that may continue to grow
with abundance.

Preface

this book "leaf's skin: seasoned poems" has consumed better part of my life.

the work is a compilation of poems and poetries that provoked curiosity, ideas and thoughts of a man in later part of his 20s.

this opus is about life how fragile it can be in moments of disturbance and how strong it can feel in moments of peace and wisdom.

"leaf's skin: seasoned poems" is a metaphor about leaves that sprout each year in early spring and when it comes fall, their withering that we pay homage to the outgoing season and welcome a new one.

leaves are like people who face life's problems with everyday but beautiful struggle, wind and its current, for and against.

how leaves change their colour and shape, its touch unfathomable like when they were young and old.

it is imperative that this work in collaboration with sharon lim sautarel will embrace each one of your expectations and needs, and of readers and connoisseurs of art.

thank you,
kumar abhishek,
poet @dr.ofletters.

Acknowledgement

i would like to express my gratitude to poets, classical and new alike, from where i've drawn inspiration and reading whom i enjoy like walt whitman, william carlos williams.

also, many thanks to the contemporary poets who have abilities that continue to mould today's literary world.

i'm also thankful to my family without whose support this was improbable.

thank you,
kumar abhishek,
poet @dr.ofletters.

TABLE OF CONTENTS

Empty Cup

one can't pour
from an empty cup

and it depends
what is poured

and what the cup
is fulfilled
up with

that it never
goes dry
in the first place

even if
it has poison

that tastes
bad,
someone toasts
a sip

but,
no.

most of us
partake interest in
the residue of the
drink in the cup

to foretell

whether you'd have a
fine time
or a
nice time.

i say where's the difference.

The Missed Clink

a clink
on
the door has

better chances

than a
knock at
the doorbell.

from
the clink

of
the glasses,

the sonorous
echo

sets
the mood.

when
a man
tries,

from
the clink

of his
woman's
bangles

emanates
liberation.

Without You

mere physical
body
feels
the existence.

and,

any day
without you
doesn’t
count.

People of Nagasaki

go away
from
the hazmat,

someone's in its vicinity.

keep distance and run,
run for your lives.

one wouldn't want
the fate of
any of
the fighters of
nagasaki.

For The Time Being

catch up with me
with conversations & ideas

but we have to
keep on jogging
and i match
your speed

jog backwards and
enhance recollection

and as you
keep
missing me,
you've been
prepared
memorable of
my close
escapes & dodges-
invisible.

if you can,
catch up
with me

if you can,
take me
down.

i'll release
you
for
the time being.

Most Real

i like you
aloof

when i'm not
provided
attention to.

that's when you're
most real.

Settled Scores

settle for less

because
sometimes

i have

more
        than
everything.

The World Owes Me, The World

i'm a rebel
who knows
the rules,
then bends them
and sometimes,
creates them

a pillar of
strength & support
if i may

keeps on giving
despite expecting
anything in return

for the people
unable to thank me
and my favors.

they're obscure
the world
owes me
a great deal,

the world.

Bulgily Relaxed

i'm relaxed
tomorrow's a day
off from work

and i have to cook
& eat
and clean
part of work,
self-work actually.

when i flourish,
i can feel
my every part and limb
bulgily relaxed.

A Swoonable Poetry

i learnt to
profess about
your beauty
& curves, my love
when i was
a school-going kid
and the words
never dare touched you.

still i write
like
a school-going kid
but you say the sex
excites only half
as much
as a swoonable poetry.

Arms Like Branches

time is my ally
and the spirit haphazardly
searches for you
places & dimensions.

both exhausted
and consumed
i have the best
of both worlds.

tell me
you are
and that you belong
in the leagues of
extraordinary.

To All My People

to all my people
here and out there,
petting
the notion
that empathy is a weakness,
then it can also be used
as a superpower
for a good cause.

you're just deprived of it yet.

Allure You In

you undermine
my courage,
like pebbles
on the roadside.

someone who collects
gemstone knows.

unlike you,
gladly i accept
in your face
i miss you
and the apologies
you loan
in the name of
thousand kisses
i take

allure you in.

As You Point Out

as you
point out,

i come to know
of my shortcomings

and there's something
in being

watched over
from a distance

the chosen few
can comprehend.

Somewhere Safe

it's a psychology
people tend to
cherish the cherries
while they're hanging
by the twigs.

things from a distance
looked after
with propensity but
when occupied neglected
like items stored
somewhere safe.

Sprout Above Beginnings

all the chaos
mood swings
sprinkles of darkness
take effect
beneath the surface
from where
the graved roots

push
and
sprout
above
beginnings
trying to touch
the sky

like your rastafarian
dreadlocks bun.

Through Thick And Thin

the sticky note
on the refrigerator
reads as:

"i'm grateful for you
to have my back
through thick
and thin."

No Ifs And Buts

good riddance
would be expensive
& fashionable worn clothings.

good riddance
would be
the golden chain
causing
itch in your neck.

good riddance
would be anything
that switched off
the mood.

Let's Be Enwrapped

like you say
we're gifted
then
let's
just
enwrap
each
other.

After Made Amends

i used to catch cold
often the high fevers
stuck with me
to even and balance
certain biased
inclinations

a free chit
to stay
in bed
after made amends
a significant repercussion
and that is
my immunity
acquires
in-built resilience.

I'm Under A Spell

i should
offer up
myself and raise
the stakes however,
i’m under a spell.

i should
be attentive
to what’s
playing however,
i’m under a spell.

i would dodge
the scorching sun
and go seek
the shadows
of trees however,
i'm under a spell.

soon i would pour
my cup of throat
with some drink
because
my famished taste buds
and my lips tell
i am
under a spell.

Who Are These Women

who are these women
with intrigued interest
to speak of me

who are these women
whose smiles
confront my headache

who are these women
show sympathy
like i need them.

who are these women
with everything
to give
and nothing to lose

who are these women
sometimes *rangoli* themselves
architecture of homes.

and who are these women
i plant a kiss
on their hands.

who are these women
know one thing and
one thing only-how
to be of compassion.

who are these women
since epoch ancience
at the forefront

and the backbone
since epoch ancience
who are these women.

The Heart And Soul of The Love Language

i imagine
we like there is
even any space
separating us.
i imagine- we and us
basic, simple yet powerful
words
wholesome ourselves
regardless the impossible.

Intricate Details

with each successive
pacific wave

touches and returns
demarcated a shoreline
my feet sunk

save sculptor
intricate details.

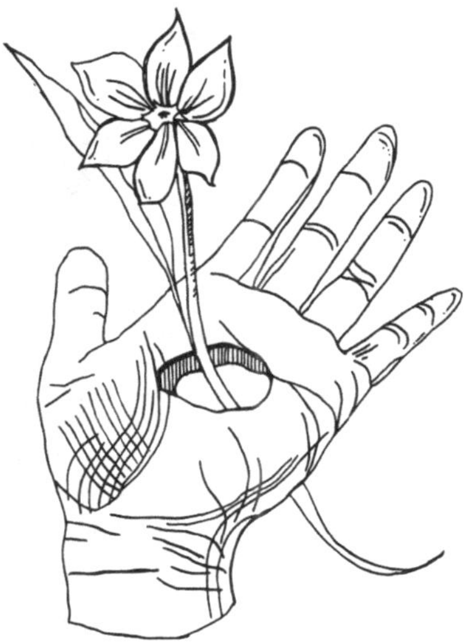

Identifying Constellations

previously i filled
inside them
colours
the pictures i got
when connected dots
now worse
like identifying
constellations.

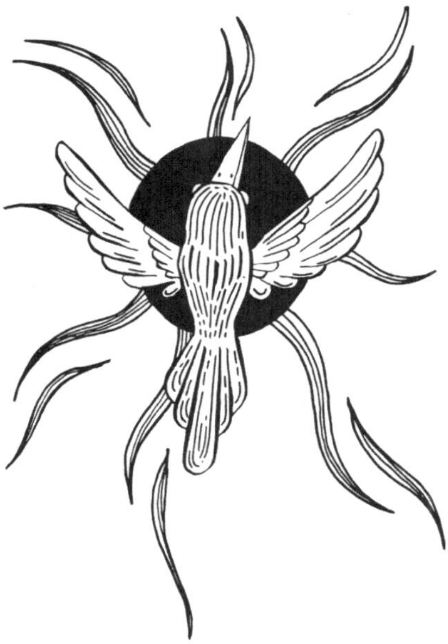

The Question

slightest of touches
arousals
or grasp tightly
like you're going
nowhere
is the question.

Demystify Conspiracy of Winters Secrecy

as some leaves
bring
change within
some leaves
assemble around all
kinds of buds help
demystify conspiracy
of winters secrecy.

My Allegiance Shifts

last night i
made you mine.
we were enough
at first alone
then together
enough like nothing
went right or
wrong
needs satiated
last night.

you look different
today in whole
new light through
mellow dancing curtains
of the room
that i'm barely
able to recognise
you and
my allegiance
shifts.

Extra Motivation

blockades are hurdles
and there's
a reason hurdle race
is a sport
in the olympics
just in case
you require
extra motivation.

That's How Long It Takes

sow a seed
take care
until it becomes
a full grown tree
and hug the trunk
and then you begin
to "love" me,
that's how long
it takes.

A Return

a hiding place
where deep fears
& dark secrets
lined-up in order
each compartmentalized
and saved.

give them
a visit
they need you.

and sometimes
mixed-up
for a recycle
tonnes of garbage
where my fears belie
i let you in
mistakenly they took
my yukata
return it
to me.

Waved At Me

i get
accustomed to
warm receptions.

everytime i'm in
my balcony

the mosses
wavy

like they waved
at me

and i blush
in return.

Bets Are Off

i spill
the beans.
i rustle
the impact
of deviations
& distractions.

i abide
by the code
else i'll lose
bets are off.

To The Top

you know what
would be perfect
a trek

with you
on my back

from where
it'd be easier
to kiss my neck.

Let Me Propose A Toast

it's immemorial
when I held
your hands
and put 'em
on my cheeks.

you're my glass
my cup
my chalice
from which
i drink.

Odds In Favour

every move
step by step
you're a promise
i kept

each day
you get better
we're in this
together.

Profound Reflection of The Self

there's some comfort
to look at someone
with unpaid attention to
while you're lost in thoughts,
and then when that
someone sees you,
lost in you.

Co-Existence

sudden gust of wind
fistful of sand
and an ocean
co-existence

you're mad
like the waves

i surf on
i splash
taken ashore
given a cpr
i'm back to life
ballistic arms
where i belong
tranquility personified.

You Sent Me Letters

you have a
bad handwriting
or so you've been
talked into.

you were willed
to fall behind
so you followed-up
stayed in-touch
sent me letters
with finest of calligraphy
and i sent you away.

Illuminating Fireflies

i have never
and would never
catch or cage
fireflies
in a mason jar

otherwise in a
pitch black darkness
that now & then
neon illumination

blip from here to there
and from there
to somewhere next

the only trail to follow
that nanosecond blip

for once it's out
and if you don't blink
it pops up further.

Old Memories

a revisit
to old memories
prayers in temples
and let
tears roll by
for journeys completed,
for journeys started.

Defenceless Yearning To Be Defeated

at your disposal
i'm disarmed
defenceless
want
to be defeated
what have you
the resources
plunge the sharp edges, love
nails, fangs, teeth
and excavate
the archeological site
yet to show surplus
battle marks
tear me apart
i'm yearning
to be defeated.

Born And Raised In Summer

after an early day,
you can doubt
my patience
and you can doubt
my strengths
maybe partake
my weakness even
crash on bed
for a home alone nap.

Oh Gawd!

the title
of this poem is
oh gawd!
and this is
the lamest
stupidest
writing, poem
you would ever
come across.

For Once

on nights
like this,

i'm poorly
exhausted
to
do
anything

like healed
injuries,
and
scars, having high
collagen than of
skin, here's reparation.

None Other Than Me

when i'm nearby

kept clandestine
by the leaves

a ripened fruit

falls from its
node

for none
other than
me.

The Ghats of Benaras

sparkling
everything
in varanasi
assi ghat
says
bienvenido
5 past 5
the ambience
a song
and
listen to
the oars
paddle
my hands
submerge
with.

Fossil

over a span

even the dead
become fossil

talk about
find a purpose

a key turned.

An Unforeseen Depth

on the surface
tip of the iceberg

other than that
the whole package

gulp responsibly
on the rocks.

Let's Take A Break

nosebleed

about time i faint

what kind of example
would be set?

that it's alright
anyone can command

or should i bypass
the extra distance?
i say
let's take a break
a head's up
down to the philtrum
ingrained red.

I Should Never Leave

i think
why i keep
coming up

i should
never leave

yet you like
my stories

and i'm
irresponsive
of your half-truths
that are half-lies

spoken like
only you
can do
my breath
devoted.

The Hints You Drop

the hints you drop
to someone to pick
and fall for you

they are gullible
about the dangerousness
forget ethics

many lost entirely

i've seen placards
in bold letters
the tagline
"missing".

I Hate You Equally

time & again
you compel me

that is to say

i hate you
equally.

One More Apology

now hush

the quiver of
lips

the unnerved coldness
sorted

allow me
to live

one more
mistake

one more
apology.

The Two of Us

your fingers
trace my face

try to exfoliate

grease and dirt

the two
of us
messier.

a hundred reasons
why complacency
welcomed

our skins
glisten

the shower
knobbed.

Salutations To The Endurance

back to square
one rejuvenate

count
the blessings

opportunities
barge in

despite
the ending

the let down
few

began
again

on the basis
of debris.

A Heart Lasted A Lifetime

created crisis

mistaken
if you're
sacrificing

misfortunes
cloud judgment.
we have been there.
leaves quite
an impression.

i'm asked
of certainty

because a heart
lasted a lifetime.

Positive Add-ons

forgiven, blessed, divinely
surplus strength
these are the terms
i want
associated with my life

to tackle the distance
arising out of
painful products
of my imagination.

i want
them dodged,
nothing else.

One Shot, One Kill

some problems

deal it with,

one shot
one kill.

A Dandelion Fluff

my problems heavier

than a dandelion fluff

spot it anywhere
& it exudes as

an unlikely source of
calmness,

a sign of good
fortune

all year 'round.

In My Life

'a day
well spent' is
a catchphrase

many years ago
i invented

i used it in
my post on
social media,

i applied it
ever since

in my life.

If Not Me

whom do i
belong to,
if not you

whom do i
assert my
feelings to,
if not you

whom do i
lay myself next to,
if not you

whom do you want if not me.

Neem

some essence

leafy veins

such spirit inside out

from barks
& stems

like lightning

that apprehends.

Lightning And Thunderstorm

you ask of tectonic plates

when's a collision

cause earthquakes

and when two
thunderclouds

talk
a revelry, a celebration
a decahedron impart.

Inside & Outside

the solus waves

simmer and dance

outside,
inwards

through the open
doors & windows

like you can see those,

the solus waves
simmer and dance.

Death And Taxes

whenever wherever

there's clashes i hit

them by the smashes

or maybe by punches

of numbers

accept the redemption

inclusive of all taxes.

A Paperclip

microsoft word's *paperclip*
got more humour
than my average
g-ds.

Beware of G-d

i stem the stamina

when i atmosphere
the g-ds
i claim virtuosity

my bargain skills
get a note of receipt.

In Equal Measure

oscillation

in a see-saw

like balance

in equal measure the
ups and downs.

Chinese Lanterns & Lamps

i am for this moment
for this moment i'm gone

the surroundings

the lights and their amps
chinese lanterns & lamps.

i am for this moment
for this moment i'm gone

the fizz brew the wiz
contained beers uncanned.

i am for this moment
for this moment i'm gone

calm & relaxed
maybe it was all pre-planned.

Call That Sahara

pour a glass of water
from the bottle of water

drink up to the throat

the glass of water

till the glass is dry

and call that *sahara.*

Aimed Rockets

israel
their citizen
over the age eighteen
must serve in
the military,
a centre of attraction

and attractive most
is the iron dome i.e.
a defensive unit
to intercept
& immobilize
aimed rockets.

Blood, Sweat And Tears

accolades,

simply elegant

the way you earn

the process you deserve

gifts
from the universe.

Lessons From The Sun

fad
is what's in trend

what's in fashion

i get what i want eventually

i have

that's why
my manifestations

give results.

I Feel Anew

jot down the excerpts
i did lately

with me it all has

i took care of 'em

they embellish me
they scintillate me

and repeatitively,
i feel anew.

Answers At Footsteps

sometimes there are *love* poems
ampersand
sometimes that evoke awareness
and provide incoming answers
to my being-
philosophical poems.

i prefer latter
as my existence is.

Invite

exceptional view
overlooked

to invite
some greater good.

GTA Vice City: Dildo Dodo

miniscule,
atomic start

so that unhindered
are little details

accumulative of them

continue with caution

to some creation

of great magnitude

like

skim the sea,
a pelican glide seaplane.

To Be A Houdini

as winter embarks,
i may need a hoodie
to be a houdini

and see what the veil
of cold has to offer
for the nights to come,

the mist good
for as far as eyes can see,
and the mist

be my favourite coalesce

afloat as i am, amongst.

Amazed

soil
    indoor plants pot
    pipes that port
    walls that
    soak heat
    i barely recollect
    these
    and look at them
    with
exclaimed,
explained
expression.

Contentment

last piece
of the jigsaw puzzle

could be the only piece

after you've inserted it,
disinterested

then let it be.

From Everything To Something

pores open
so that
the light must
efface them
could be anything

from broken haunted mansions,
to mending souls

from the rainforest
to an emerging seedling,
to its tiny leaf

from everything,
to something.

I Raise A Glass

the things of the past,
are past

to show that i've got class
i raise a glass

a cup to the heaven(s)

so that i'm bestowed
with the present
that i get.

Wobble Head

of an action figure

wobble-head

nod

come what may
always eager.

As Per The Needs

in order to be,

cultivate surroundings

the things in them

as per the needs

so that

i belong.

Logic Behind Botany

involvement necessary

when it comes to nature

a nursery that nourishes

garden of soul.

For Adulthood And Hunting

a sail on ice

i sleigh clear
of problems

a polar bear
parenting skills
make me

for adulthood
and hunting.

In Need of Finesse

in need of finesse,
there is cherry on top of a cake
there is portrait of an image
there are clothings on a body
there are fine men to a healthy discussion
there is cultural well-being
and its festivities to a society.

a map by the explorer.

Audio Casette

a cassette

from the 70s

playlist emerges

encyclopedia
of feelings

love lost
or found.

Moral Cleanse

for placement of things
like a cup of coffee,
a cup of tea

by a window of books
in a room
a table is important

such as
legs to walk
eyes to see.

Elements

basic elements
are five

earth, water, air, fire, space-
the basis of things

all of them natural
than man-made.

Made of Palm Leaf

made of palm leaf

a fan

i swing it for
these sweat
beads

down to the cheeks
and chin

cool and glazy
skin.

A Persian Poetry

sandclock hourglass

grain by grain

one by one

upside down,
continuum
a quicksand.

Inside, A Postcard

a postal stamp
on a square envelope

inside,
a *postcard* worth
thousand smiles.

To Fulfil The Calling

steady study

one has to,

to fulfill the calling

so that the night
invests its interests.

Good Things

jumps on trampoline,
never stop

just like
good things

arrive late.

Patience

tested with
patience of
the season,
latest fruits.

In The Savannas

enjoyment is a
necessity for survival,

even in the
savannas.

Daily Kept Scrapbook

with a small pair of scissors

just fit for the newspaper cut

corner-by-corner
the images

to be gummed

in a daily kept scrapbook.

Coming of Age

in the middle of an empire,

pollens

due to be outside

protection of petals

coming of age

they'd precise an ode
of a giver.

This And Other Directions

at yellow traffic light,

vehicles and automobiles

some to go straight

some have their indicators
flashing left

some would steer right.

Sounds Reach To Ears In Waves

nails strumm strings

a blend of
altitudinal highs

and lows like

in a visualizer

an environ
an ambience
enjoyment.

Propelling Wings

in a millennia a shooting star
took care of business itself,
a life transformed
propelling wings of a butterfly.

A Yummy Scenario

i peeled and i held
a ripe mango
my teeth plunge
and scoop a bite of it

delicious psychedelic fun
a gleeful tingle.

A Different Angle

they are still there-

a jar of lemon pickles,
an used appy fizz bottle,
an aloe vera plant pottery
with centimetres of mint herbs in it.

it's just that i looked at them
from a different angle.

Plugged

just like certain electronics
need charging

my spiritual side
also needs
to be plugged.

To Me

to me,
    they bring luck

    special

    autumn maple leaves

    even the one
    about to fly beside
    on the bench

    more than sufficient.

Epilogue

this book is in collaboration with sharon lim sautarel who never fails to amaze her audience with her illustrations and sketches.

it is about patience of the humbly rooted trees, down to earth their occupation.

it is about opening your heart to nature, especially trees, and how their leaves make them whole and unique like type of clothings bode on them.

just like anyone, it focuses on leaves and their journey each year from beginning to end or vice-versa, a recurring cycle

telling us of a walk in immersion of nature is completely enough.

9 789334 151954

Printed at Repro India Ltd.